AF292607

RATKO DELORKO

Zappelige Muzik: 24 +1 Unstete Klavierstücke

Fidgety Muzic: 24 +1 Restless Pieces For Piano

Vorwiegend für Menschen mit AHDS

Primarily for people with ADHD

ZK 5275

Zappelige Muzik: 24 +1 Unstete Klavierstücke
Fidgety Muzic: 24 +1 Restless Pieces For Piano

24 +1 unstete Klavierstücke

Menschen mit ADHS (Aufmerksamkeitsdefizit-Hyperaktivitätsstörung) können von speziell konzipierter Musik profitieren, die ihnen hilft, sich besser zu konzentrieren, sich zu beruhigen oder ihre kognitiven Funktionen zu stimulieren. Oder sich einfach nur im musikalischem Spiegel zu betrachten. Im Vorfeld habe ich die spezifischen Anforderungen und Vorlieben von Menschen mit ADHS in Bezug auf Musik untersucht.

Die Maßgeschneiderte Komposition: Ich schrieb eine Serie von Klavierstücken, die speziell darauf abzielen, Konzentration und Fokus bei ADHS-Betroffenen zu fördern und deren stark verkürzten Aufmerksamkeitsspanne Rechnung tragen mit der Integration von rhythmischen und harmonischen Elementen, die beruhigend wirken oder motorisch so angelegt sind, Ablenkungen zu kanalisieren bzw. reduzieren.

Die Entwicklung von Musik speziell für Spieler mit ADHS kann eine innovative Methode darstellen, um die Konzentration und das Spielerlebnis dieser Zielgruppe zu verbessern.

Es ist wichtig zu wissen, dass nicht alle Menschen mit ADHS auf Musik in der gleichen Weise reagieren werden. Einige werden einen bestimmten Kompositionsstil bevorzugen, während andere dies nicht tun. Es kann sinnvoll sein, auch gegensätzliche Anlagen von Musik auszuprobieren, um herauszufinden, welche am besten für den individuellen Spieler oder Zuhörer funktioniert. deswegen entwickelt dieser Klavierzyklus sehr unterschiedliche Ansätze und Ausprägungen.

24 +1 Restless Piano Pieces

People with ADHD (Attention Deficit Hyperactivity Disorder) may benefit from specially designed music to help them concentrate better, calm down, or stimulate their cognitive functions. Or just look at themself in the musical mirror. In advance, I examined the specific requirements and preferences of people with ADHD in relation to music.

The tailor-made composition: I was creating a series of piano pieces that are specifically aimed at promoting concentration and focus in those affected by ADHD and take into account their greatly shortened attention span with the integration of rhythmic and harmonic elements that have a calming effect or are designed to be motor-specific in order to channel or reduce distractions.

Developing music specifically for people with ADHD can be an innovative way to improve concentration and the musical experience for this target group.

It's important to note that not all people with ADHD will respond to music in the same way. Some will benefit from a particular composition style while others will not. It can make sense to try out different styles of music to find out which works best for the individual player / listener. That's why this piano cycle develops very different approaches and characteristics.

Imprint ISBN 978-3-384-10145-7

Music:	© 2023	Copyright by Ratko Delorko
Text:	© 2023	Copyright by Ratko Delorko
Pictures:	© 2023	Copyright by Ratko Delorko
Content:	Ratko Delorko Zeitklang	
	Eichendorffstr. 31	
	45219 Essen zeitklangmedia@gmx.de	www.delorko.com
Print:	Tredition, Hamburg	

ZAPPELIGE MUZIK: 24 +1 UNSTETE KLAVIERSTÜCKE
FIDGETY MUZIC: 24 +1 RESTLESS PIECES FOR PIANO

Violett, türkis, orange, rot.
Purple, Turquoise, Orange, Red.

Ratko Delorko

7
21
25
29
pp
*
15ma
33
f
ff
Ped.
Ped.
loco
diminuendo
37
3
41
pp
mf
3 2 1
* 01:15

Räume nicht meinen Schreibtisch auf!
Don't clean up my desk!

Ratko Delorko

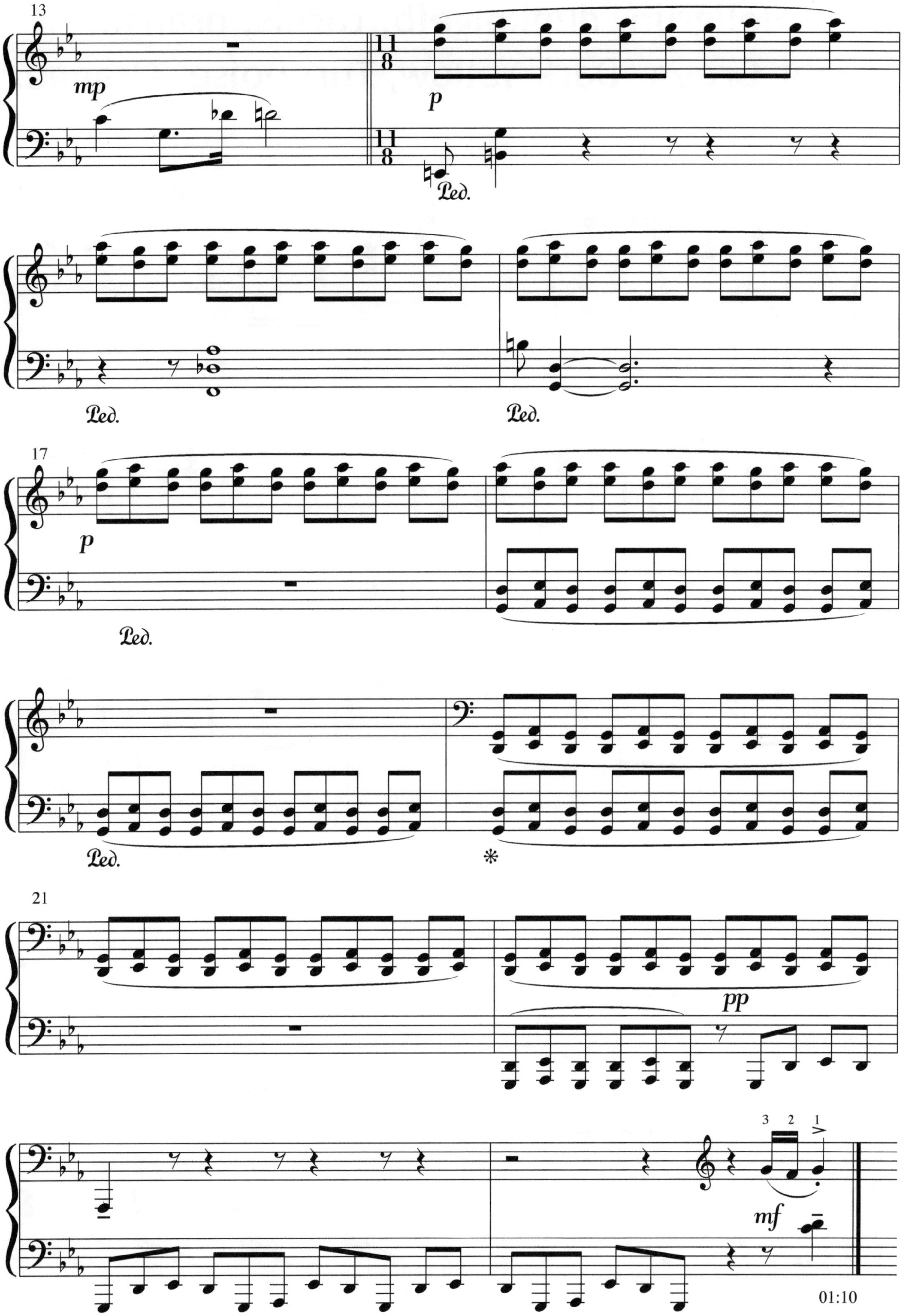
13
mp
11
8
p
Ped.
Ped.
Ped.
17
p
Ped.
Ped.
*
21
pp
3 2 1
mf

01:10

Hellgrün, dunkelgelb, türkis, orange.
Light Green, Dark Yellow, Turquoise, Orange.

Ratko Delorko

13
p
Ped. Ped.
17
p
Ped. Ped. Ped.
21
Ped. Ped. Ped. Ped.
25
Ped. Ped. Ped. Ped. Ped.
f
Ped. Ped. *

12
29
3
2/4
3/4
33
3/4
3
2/4
Led.
Led.
2/4
1 2 4
3/4
37
3 2 3
Led.
Led.
Led.
Led.
Led.
4/4
4/4
Led.
Led.
41
4/4
4/4
p
Led.
Led.
Led.
Led.
Led.
Led.
45
a tempo
3 2 1
poco rit.
ppp
ff
mf
3/16
3/16
Led.
Led.
Led.
Led.
01:40

Königsblau
Royal Blue

Ratko Delorko

14
loco
13
8va
15ma
Ped.
15ma
sfz
loco
17
Ped.
3 2 1
mf
Sost.
Ped.
0:33

Schätzen, wie viel Schlaf ich bekommen würde, wenn ich jetzt einschlafen könnte.

Bitte seien Sie creativ und entwickeln Ihre eigene Dynamik.

Estimating the Amount of Sleep I Would Receive if I Could Just "Fall Asleep Right Now."

Get creative and develop your own dynamics, please

Ratko Delorko

11
12
13
14
15
16
17
18
19
20
21
22
23
24
25
26
Ped.
Ped.
Ped.
Ped.
Ped.
Ped.
Ped.
Ped.

Ped.
Ped.
Ped.
Ped.
Ped.
8va
rallentando
a tempo
01:10

Rechts? Links?
Right? Left?

Ratko Delorko

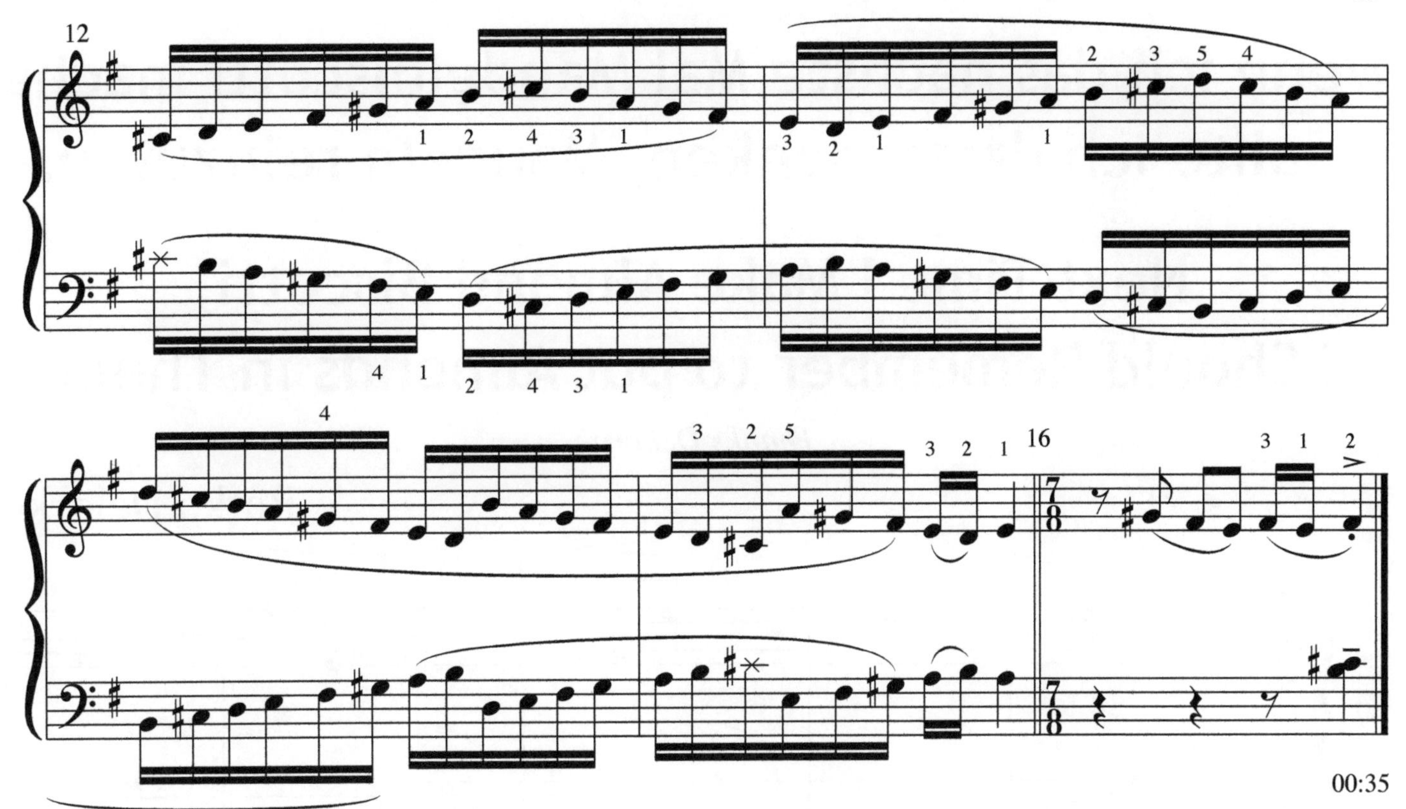

12
16
00:35

Wenn ich das nächste Mal Mandelbiscotti mache, sollte ich daran denken, Mandeln reinzutun.

Next Time I Make Almond Biscotti, I Should Remember to put Almonds in Them.

Thanks Deborah

Ratko Delorko

Türkis, rot, orange.
Turquoise, Red, Orange.

Alles so schön bunt hier...
Everything is so Colorful Here...

Ratko Delorko

23
13
5
17
f
p
f
mf
mf
Ped.
Ped.
Ped.
Ped.
Ped.
21

37
8va bassa
Ped.
loco
Ped.
41
mp
Ped.
Ped.
Ped.
Ped.
Ped.
45
Thank you Mr. Bach:
Ped.
Ped.
Ped.
ff
sfz
mf
Ped.
01:35

Vergesslichkeit
Forgetfulness

Ratko Delorko

Ständiges Gezappel
Constantly Fidgeting

Ratko Delorko

28
mp
mf
f
mf
13
mf
♩=120
3   3
f
Ped.   *
3   3
3 2 1
mf
Ped.   *
00:40

Gelbe, orange und weisse Murmeln
Yellow, Orange, and White Marbles

Ratko Delorko

Alles verlegt
All Misplaced

Ratko Delorko

Der Versuch ruhig zu bleiben
The Attempt to Keep Calm

Ratko Delorko

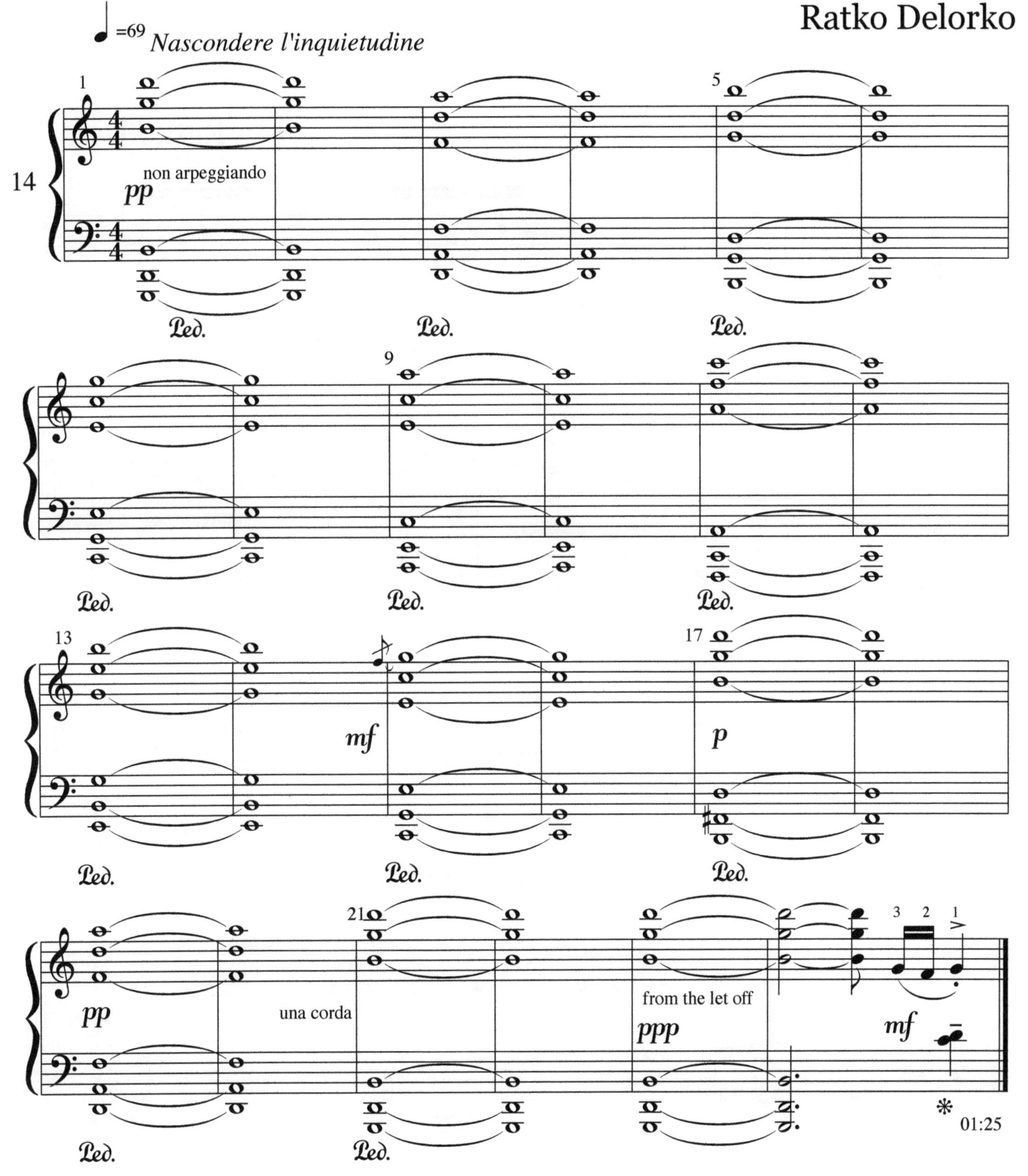

Bring mein Durcheinander nicht durcheinander!
Don't mess with my mess!

Ratko Delorko

Ped.
Ped.
Ped.
Ped.
Ped.
Ped.
f
mf
p
pp
m.d.
mf
00:50

Dinge fallen lassen
Dropping Things

Ratko Delorko

35
13
una corda
p
Ped.
17
tre corde
f
8va bassa
Ped.
Ped.
loco
8va bassa
Ped.
Ped.
Ped.
Ped.
21
mf
3
p
3
25
mf
3 1 2
00:50

Gezappel
Fidget

Ratko Delorko

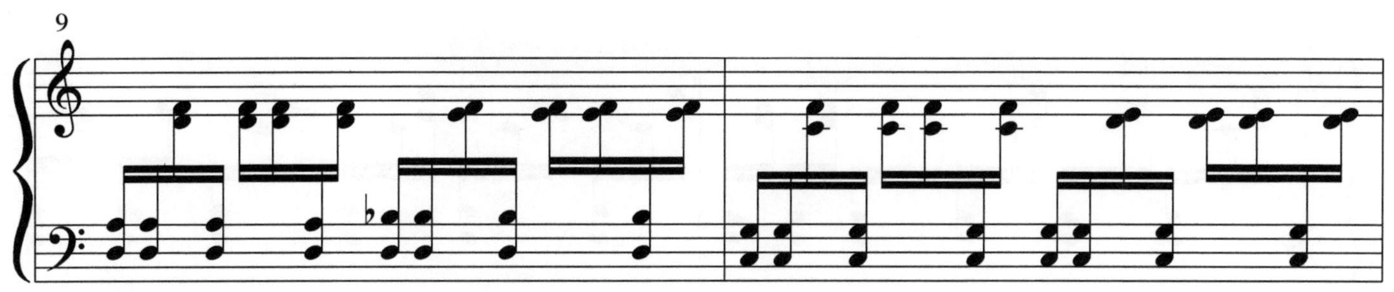

21
Ped. *
f
Ped. * Ped. *
25
cresc.
ff
mf
3 2 1
Ped. Ped. *
00:50

€
0.50
€
0.50

Unterbrechen
Interrupting

Ratko Delorko

25
p
Ped.
Ped.
29
mf
33
37
p
3
p
3
mf
3
41
Ped.
00:52

Nebel im Kopf
Brain Fog

Ratko Delorko

43
8va
13
8va
8va
loco
5
4
5
4
3
2
1
a tempo
veloce
rallentando
p
loco 1
1
2
1
2
1
Ped.
17
Ped.
Ped.
Ped.
Ped.
21
pp
Ped.
Ped.
una corda
Ped.
Ped.
25
4
2
3
mf
Ped.
Ped.
Ped.
tre corde
01:50

Vor und zurück, keine Entscheidung
Back and Forth, no Decision

Ratko Delorko

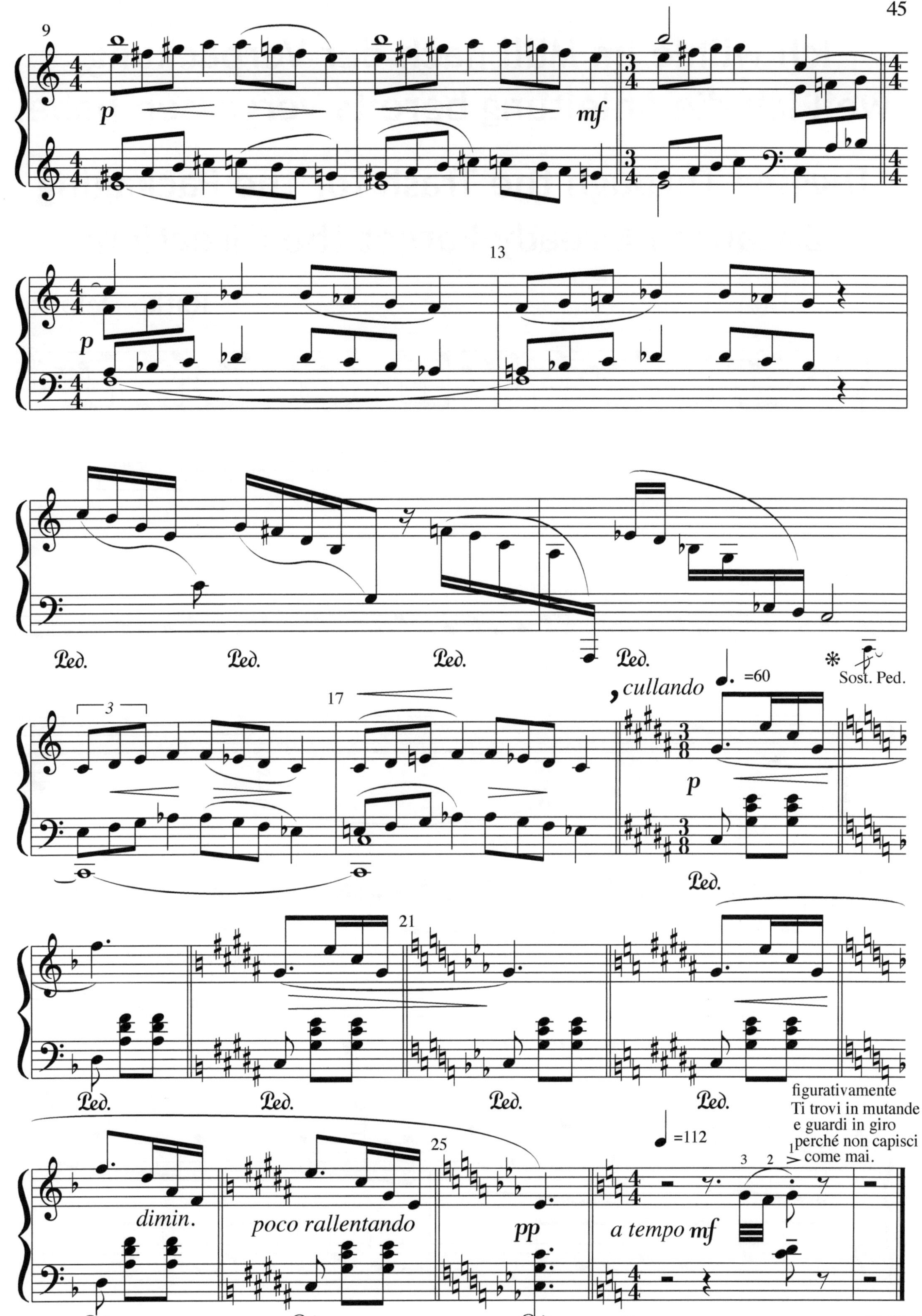
p
mf
13
p
Ped.
Ped.
Ped.
Ped.
cullando
♩.=60
Sost. Ped.
3
17
p
Ped.
21
Ped.
Ped.
Ped.
Ped.
figurativamente
Ti trovi in mutande
e guardi in giro
perché non capisci
come mai.
♩=112
25
dimin.
poco rallentando
pp
a tempo mf
Ped.
Ped.
Ped.

Ich wühle im Müll nach der Verpackung, weil ich die Anleitung bereits vergessen habe.

Digging Through the Trash for the Packaging Because I Already Forgot the Directions.

Ratko Delorko

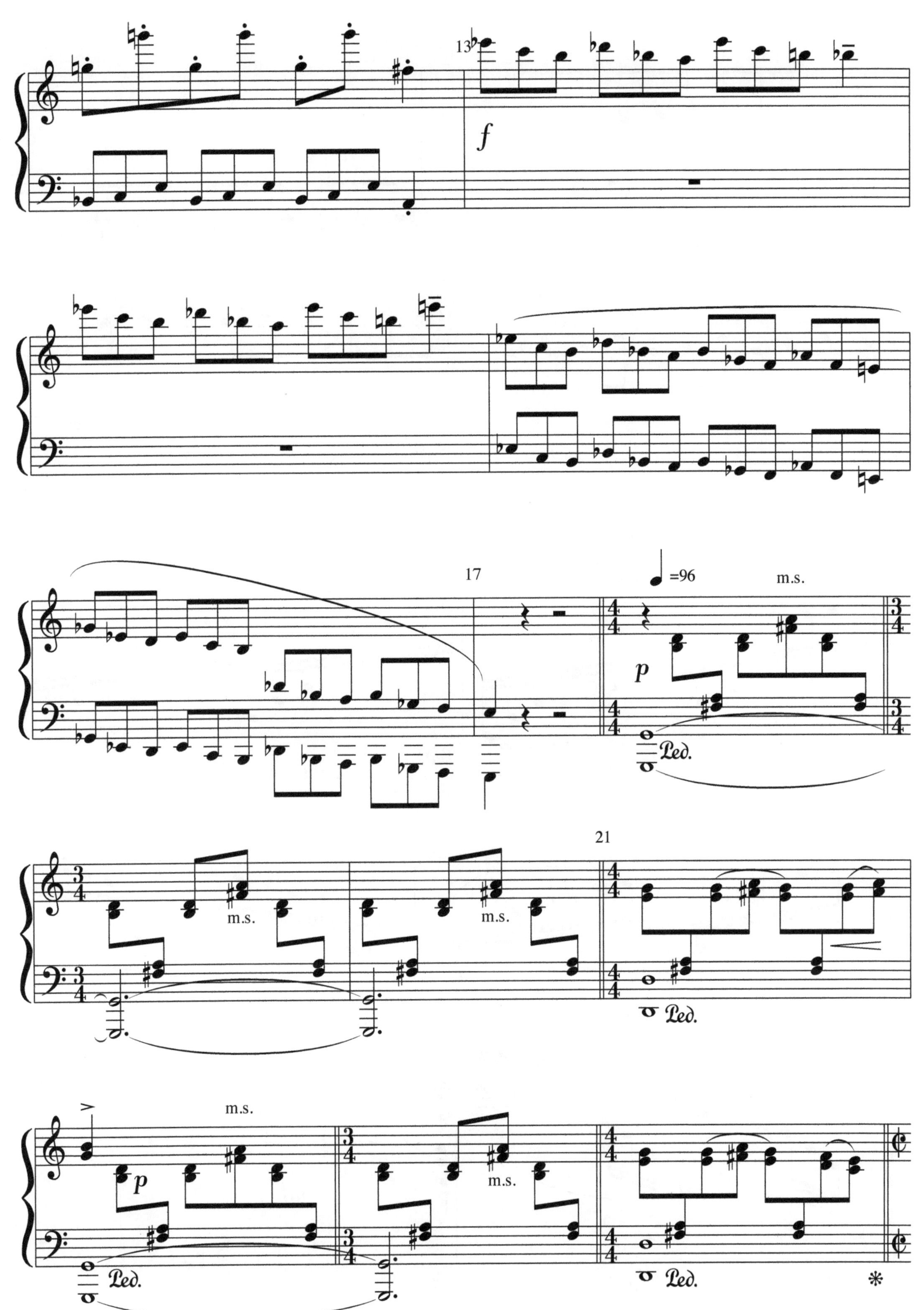
f
13
=96
m.s.
p
m.s.
Ped.
m.s.
m.s.
Ped.
21
m.s.
p
Ped.
m.s.
Ped.

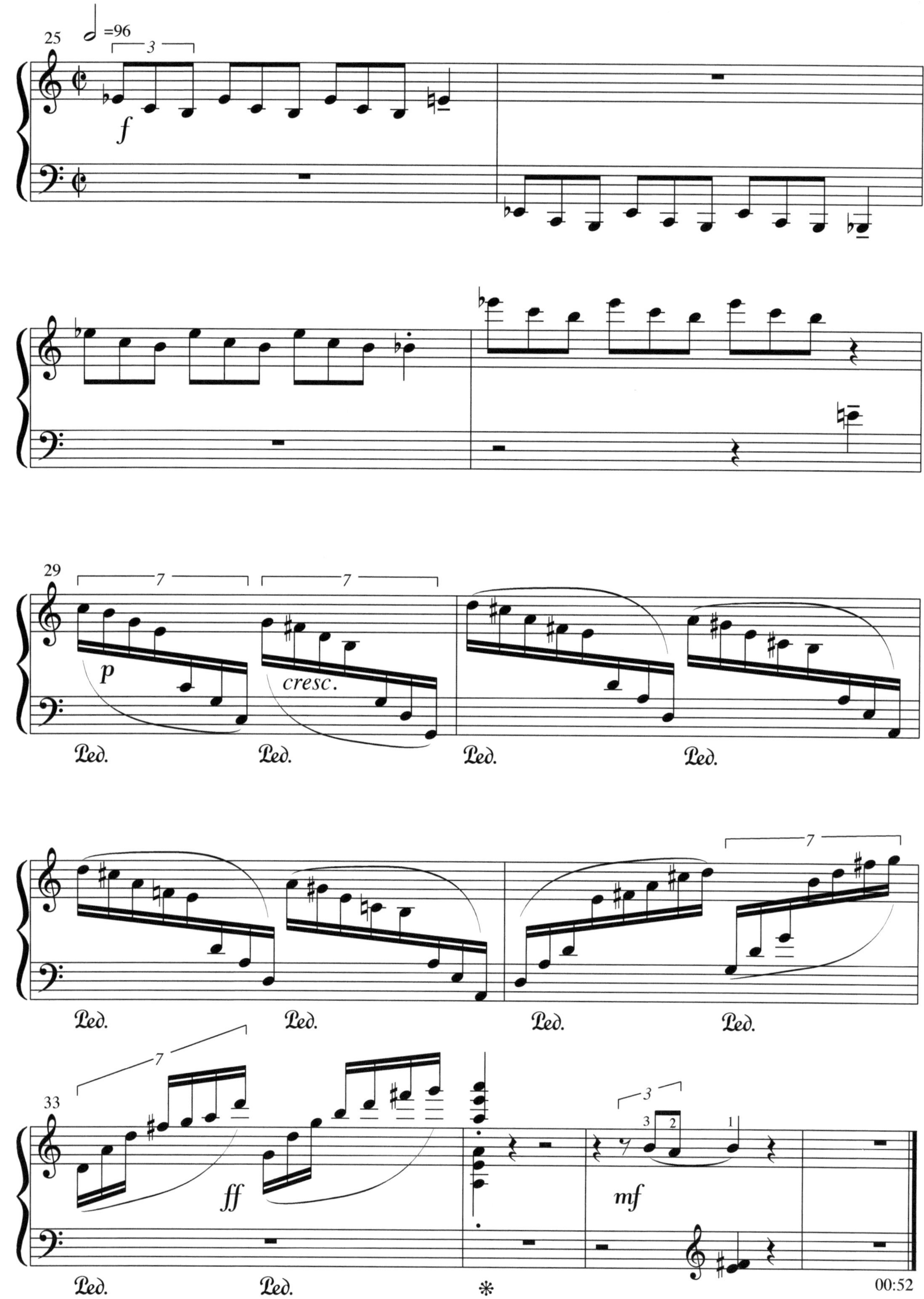

48
25
♩=96
3
f
29
7
7
p
cresc.
Ped.
Ped.
Ped.
Ped.
Ped.
Ped.
Ped.
Ped.
33
7
7
3
3
2
1
ff
mf
Ped.
Ped.
*
00:52

Pläne schmieden. Um dann sogleich zu bedauern, geplant zu haben.

Making Plans.
Then Immediately Regretting Making Plans.

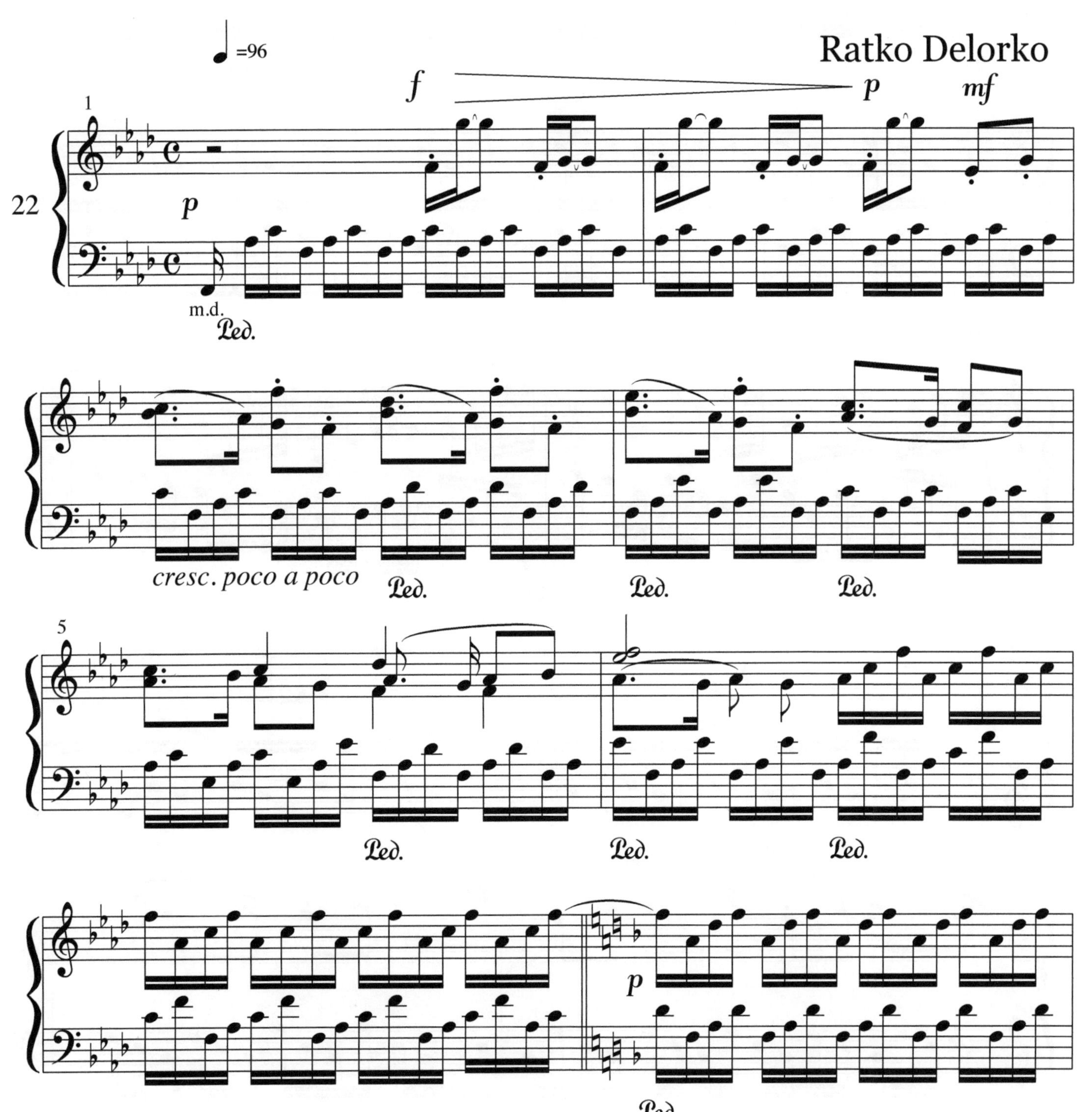

50
cresc. poco a poco
Ped.
Ped.
Ped.
Ped.
Ped.
15ma
loco
f
Ped.
Ped.
f
p
mf
p
Ped.
Ped.
Ped.
Ped.

51
21
Ped. Ped.
Ped. Ped. Ped. Ped.
5 sec.
25
Ped. *
3 sec.
mf
3 3
29
p senza emozione
Ped. *
33 3 37
mf
p
Ped. Ped. Ped. Ped. * Ped. Ped. Ped. Ped. *
02::10

Fuge über A D H Es
Fugue on A D H D

Ratko Delorko

25
53
29
33
37
41
45
3
3 2 1
3
01:30

Grün, braun, rot, Flieder, gelb, weiss.
Green, Brown, Red, Lilac, Yellow, White.

Ratko Delorko

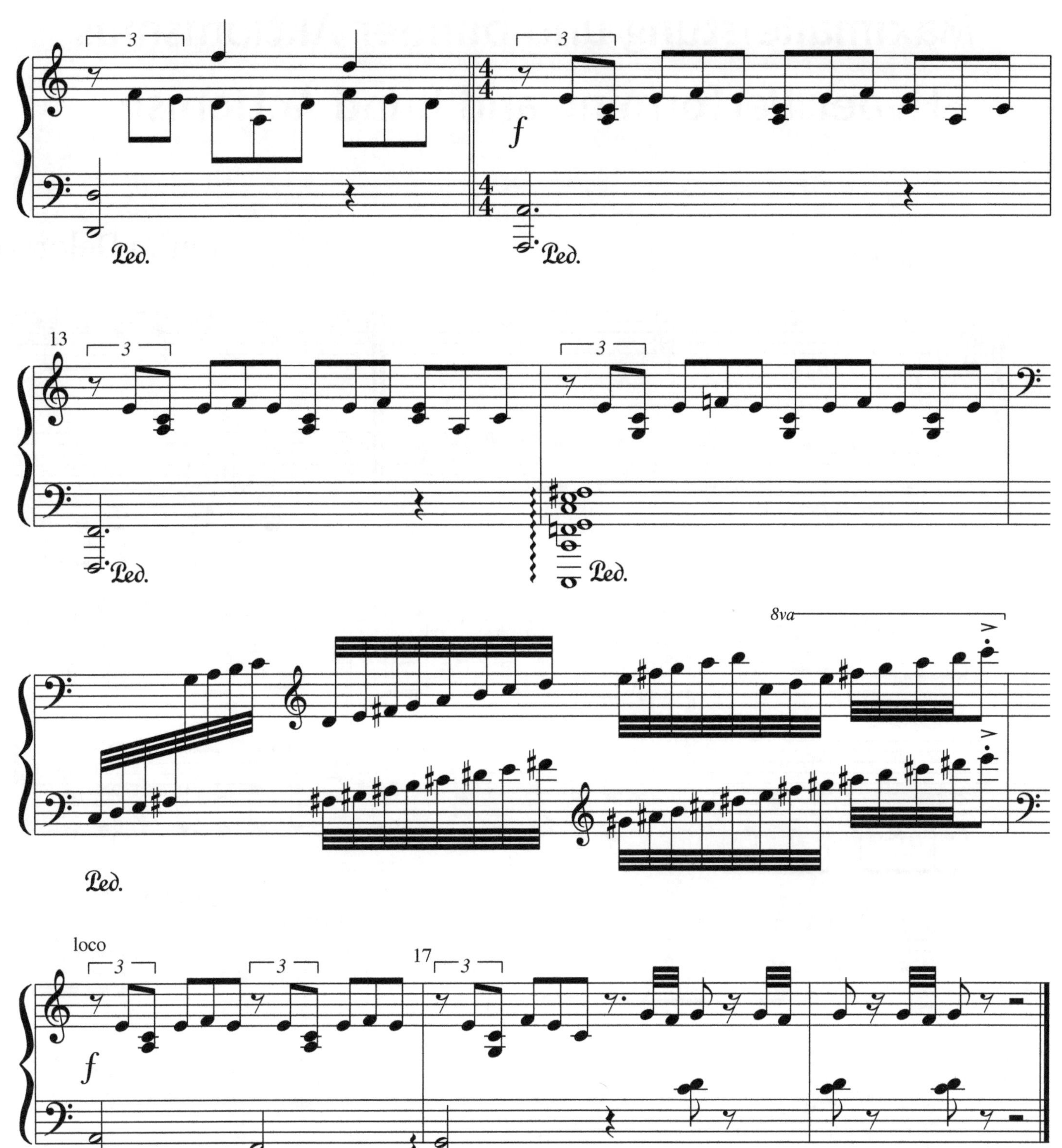

3
3
4
4
f
Ped.
Ped.
13
3
3
Ped.
Ped.
8va
loco
3
3
17
3
f
Ped.
Ped.
Ped.
01:10

Maximalleistung und blinder Aktionismus
Hyper Performing and Blind Actionism

57
13
p
cresc.
f
17
3/4
♩=112
21
3/4
4/4
mf
sfz
ff
25
3
Ped. Ped. Ped. Ped. Ped. Ped. Ped. Ped. * Ped.
8va bassa
01:05
*

 **Notes**